I0528572

**The Walker and Mason Guide to
The Mid-Century Modern Dinner Party**

ISBN 978-1-989647-29-5

© 2023 R.H.Mason

A Byrd Press Publication
Toronto
www.byrdpress.com
publisher@byrdpress.com

cover design R.H. Mason
interior art Felipe Silva

The Walker and Mason Guide to

The Mid-Century Modern Dinner Party

Step into the captivating world of mid-century modern cuisine, where each recipe is a portal to an era defined by sophistication, innovation, and a dash of retro charm. In this culinary journey, we revisit the glamorous dinner parties, the artful presentation of dishes, and the eclectic mix of flavors that graced the tables of the mid-20th century. From classic cocktails that echo the clinking glasses of glamorous gatherings to appetizers and desserts that showcase the culinary trends of the time, this book invites you to savor the past while embracing the present. Join us as we rediscover the magic of mid-century modern cooking—a feast for the senses and a celebration of an era where every meal was a symphony of flavors and every dinner party an unforgettable event. Welcome to a time capsule of taste, where the spirit of the mid-century is served on every plate.

TABLE OF CONTENTS.

The Cocktails.

The Recipes.

THE
COCKTAILS

20 Unique Cocktails Inspired by the Mid-Century Modern Era

1. Martini à la Mad Men

Ingredients:
- 2 oz gin
- 1/2 oz dry vermouth
- Lemon twist for garnish

Instructions:
1. Stir gin and dry vermouth with ice.
2. Strain into a chilled martini glass.
3. Garnish with a lemon twist.

Transport yourself to the Mad Men era with this classic and sleek Martini, served just the way they liked it.

2. Whiskey Smash:

Ingredients:
- 2 oz bourbon or rye whiskey
- 3/4 oz simple syrup
- Fresh mint leaves
- Lemon wedge for garnish

Instructions:
1. Muddle mint and simple syrup in a glass.
2. Add whiskey and ice, then shake.
3. Strain into a rocks glass over ice.
4. Garnish with a lemon wedge.

Savor the refreshing simplicity of a Whiskey Smash with its vibrant mix of mint and citrus.

3. Mai Tai Revival:

Ingredients:
- 2 oz aged rum
- 3/4 oz fresh lime juice
- 1/2 oz orange liqueur
- 1/2 oz orgeat syrup
- 1/4 oz simple syrup
- Orange twist for garnish

Instructions:
1. Shake all ingredients with ice.
2. Strain into a rocks glass filled with crushed ice.
3. Garnish with an orange twist.

Experience the vibrant revival of a classic Mai Tai with this well-balanced and flavorful concoction.

4. Gimlet Twist:

Ingredients:
- 2 oz gin
- 3/4 oz elderflower liqueur
- 1/2 oz lime juice
- Fresh basil leaves

Instructions:
1. Muddle a few fresh basil leaves in a shaker.
2. Add gin, elderflower liqueur, and lime juice.
3. Shake well with ice.

4. Strain into a chilled martini glass.
5. Garnish with a basil leaf.

Enjoy the herbal infusion of basil in this delightful twist on the classic Gimlet. Cheers!

5. Pink Squirrel:

Ingredients:
- 1 oz creme de noyaux
- 1 oz white creme de cacao
- 1 oz heavy cream

Instructions:
1. Shake all ingredients with ice.
2. Strain into a chilled cocktail glass.
3. Garnish with a cherry.

Indulge in the sweet and nutty delight of the Pink Squirrel, a classic cocktail with a charming pink hue.

6. Vesper Royale:

Ingredients:
- 2 oz gin
- 1 oz vodka
- 1/2 oz Lillet Blanc
- Lemon twist for garnish

Instructions:
1. Stir gin, vodka, and Lillet Blanc with ice.
2. Strain into a chilled coupe glass.
3. Garnish with a twist of lemon.

Elevate the classic Vesper with a touch
of sophistication in the Vesper Royale.

7. Ginger Bee's Knees:

Ingredients:
- 2 oz gin
- 3/4 oz honey syrup (1:1 honey and water)
- 1/2 oz fresh lemon juice
- 1/4 oz ginger syrup

Instructions:
1. Shake all ingredients with ice.
2. Strain into a chilled coupe glass.
3. Garnish with a twist of lemon.

Savor the delightful combination of gin,
honey, and a hint of ginger in this
refreshing Ginger Bee's Knees cocktail.

8. Tequila Sunrise Revival:

Ingredients:
- 2 oz high-quality tequila
- 1 oz blood orange liqueur
- 1/2 oz agave syrup
- 3/4 oz fresh lime juice
- 1 oz pomegranate juice
- 1/2 oz passion fruit puree
- 1 dash orange bitters
- Orange slice and edible flowers for
garnish

Instructions:
1. In a shaker, combine tequila, blood
orange liqueur, agave syrup, fresh lime
juice, pomegranate juice, passion fruit

puree, and a dash of orange bitters.
2. Shake well with ice.
3. Strain into a tall glass filled with ice.
4. Slowly pour the pomegranate juice over the back of a spoon or by drizzling it down the side of the glass to create a layered effect.
5. Garnish with an orange slice and edible flowers.

Experience the vibrant and layered flavors of this Complex Tequila Sunrise Revival, a contemporary twist on the classic sunrise cocktail.

9. Aviation:

Ingredients:
- 2 oz gin
- 1/2 oz maraschino liqueur
- 1/2 oz creme de violette
- 3/4 oz fresh lemon juice
- Maraschino cherry for garnish

Instructions:
1. Shake gin, maraschino liqueur, creme de violette, and fresh lemon juice with ice.
2. Strain into a chilled martini glass.
3. Garnish with a maraschino cherry.

Embark on a journey of elegance with the Aviation cocktail, where the floral notes of creme de violette complement the classic gin and citrus blend. Cheers!

10. Pisco Sour:

Ingredients:
- 2 oz pisco
- 3/4 oz elderflower liqueur
- 1 oz fresh lemon juice
- 1/2 oz simple syrup
- 1/2 oz dry vermouth
- 1 egg white
- Angostura bitters for garnish

Instructions:
1. Dry shake (shake without ice) pisco, elderflower liqueur, fresh lemon juice, simple syrup, dry vermouth, and egg white vigorously for about 10 seconds.
2. Add ice and shake again for another 10 seconds.
3. Strain into a chilled coupe glass.
4. Garnish with a few drops of Angostura bitters, creating a decorative pattern.

Delight in the complexity of flavors and the frothy texture in this elevated rendition of the classic Pisco Sour.

11. Boulevardier:

Ingredients:
- 1 1/2 oz bourbon
- 1 oz sweet vermouth
- 1 oz Campari
- Orange twist for garnish

Instructions:
1. Stir bourbon, sweet vermouth, and Campari with ice.

2. Strain into a chilled rocks glass over a large ice cube.
3. Express the oil from an orange twist over the drink and drop it in.

Savor the sophisticated bitterness of the Boulevardier, a timeless cocktail reminiscent of a Negroni but with the warmth of bourbon.

12. Sidecar Redux:

Ingredients:
- 2 oz cognac
- 3/4 oz triple sec
- 1/2 oz Cointreau
- 1 oz fresh lemon juice
- 1/2 oz honey syrup (1:1 honey and water)
- 1 dash orange bitters
- Edible gold flakes for garnish (optional)

Instructions:
1. Shake cognac, triple sec, Cointreau, fresh lemon juice, honey syrup, and a dash of orange bitters with ice.
2. Double strain into a chilled coupe glass.
3. Garnish with a sprinkle of edible gold flakes for a touch of luxury.

Indulge in the rich and nuanced flavors of this Complex and Elevated Sidecar Redux, a modern twist on the classic cocktail with added depth and sophistication.

13. Tropical Tease:

Ingredients:
- 2 oz coconut rum

- 1/2 oz banana liqueur
- 3 oz pineapple juice
- Squeeze of fresh lime

Instructions:

1. Fill a shaker with ice.
2. Add coconut rum, banana liqueur, pineapple juice, and a squeeze of fresh lime.
3. Shake well and strain into a chilled glass over ice.
4. Garnish with a pineapple wedge.

Indulge in the exotic allure of the Tropical Tease, blending coconut, banana, and citrus for a refreshing and tropical escape.

14. Paloma Fresca:

Ingredients:
- 2 oz blanco tequila
- 1 oz fresh grapefruit juice
- 1/2 oz fresh lime juice
- 1/2 oz agave syrup
- Club soda
- Grapefruit wedge for garnish
- Tajín or salt for rimming (optional)

Instructions:
1. Rim a highball glass with Tajín or salt (optional).
2. Fill the glass with ice.
3. In a shaker, combine tequila, fresh grapefruit juice, fresh lime juice, and agave syrup. Shake well.

4. Strain the mixture over the ice in the glass.
5. Top with club soda.
6. Garnish with a grapefruit wedge.
Enjoy the bright and refreshing Paloma Fresca, a lively tequila cocktail
that captures the essence of citrus and agave sweetness.

15. Rusty Nail Remastered:

Ingredients:
- 2 oz high-end single malt Scotch whisky
- 1 oz premium honey liqueur
- A few drops of rare and aged bitters
- Ice sphere made from artisanal water
- Gold-infused honeycomb for garnish

Instructions:
1. In a crystal mixing glass, combine the exquisite Scotch whisky, honey
liqueur, and drops of rare bitters.
2. Stir gently with a gold-plated bar spoon.
3. Strain the elixir into a tumbler over a meticulously crafted ice sphere.
4. Garnish with a delicate, gold-infused honeycomb.

Savor the opulence of the Rusty Nail Remastered, where each
element is a testament to the artistry of fine spirits. This elevated version
transcends tradition, offering a truly luxurious drinking experience.

16. Tom Collins Twist:

Ingredients:
- 2 oz gin
- 3/4 oz elderflower liqueur
- 1 oz fresh lemon juice
- 1/2 oz simple syrup
- A handful of fresh basil leaves
- Club soda
- Lemon wheel for garnish

Instructions:
1. In a shaker, muddle fresh basil leaves with gin, elderflower liqueur, fresh lemon juice, and simple syrup.
2. Shake well with ice.
3. Strain into a Collins glass filled with ice.
4. Top with club soda.
5. Garnish with a lemon wheel and a sprig of fresh basil.

Elevate the classic Tom Collins with the aromatic freshness of basil and the floral notes of elderflower. This Tom Collins Twist is a delightful and sophisticated sipper.

17. Harvey Wallbanger 2.0:

Ingredients:
- 2 oz vodka
- 3/4 oz Galliano
- 1 oz fresh orange juice
- 1/2 oz vanilla-infused simple syrup
- 1/2 oz lavender-infused liqueur
- Orange zest for garnish
- Edible flower petals for garnish

Instructions:
1. In a shaker, combine vodka, Galliano, fresh orange juice, vanilla-infused simple syrup, and lavender-infused liqueur.
2. Shake well with ice.
3. Strain into a highball glass filled with ice.
4. Garnish with a twist of orange zest and a sprinkle of edible flower petals.

Experience the avant-garde Harvey Wallbanger 2.0, enriched with the unexpected combination of vanilla and lavender for a uniquely aromatic and floral twist.

18. Rum Swizzle:

Ingredients:
- 1 1/2 oz 151-proof dark rum
- 1 oz pineapple juice
- 1 oz orange juice
- 3/4 oz falernum
- 1/2 oz passion fruit syrup
- 1/2 oz lime juice
- 1/4 oz grenadine
- Crushed ice
- Pineapple wedge and mint sprig for garnish

Instructions:
1. Fill a tiki mug or highball glass with crushed ice.
2. In a shaker, combine 151-proof dark rum, pineapple juice, orange juice,

falernum, passion fruit syrup, lime juice,
and grenadine.
3. Shake well and pour over the crushed
ice in the glass.
4. Swizzle the mixture with a swizzle stick
or bar spoon until well-chilled.
5. Garnish with a pineapple wedge and a
sprig of mint.

Transport yourself to the tropics with
the intense 151 Rum Swizzle, a signature
concoction from the world of tiki bars.

19. Negroni Sbagliato:

Ingredients:
- 1 oz Campari
- 1 oz sweet vermouth
- 3 oz prosecco (or other sparkling wine)
- Orange slice for garnish

Instructions:
1. Fill a rocks glass with ice.
2. Pour Campari and sweet vermouth over
the ice.
3. Top with prosecco.
4. Stir gently.
5. Garnish with an orange slice.

Indulge in the bubbly sophistication of the
Negroni Sbagliato, a delightful variation
of the classic Negroni with the
effervescence of prosecco.

20. Zombie Punch:

Ingredients:
- 1 1/2 oz aged Jamaican rum
- 1 oz overproof rum (151-proof)
- 1/2 oz apricot liqueur
- 1/2 oz falernum
- 3/4 oz cinnamon syrup
- 3/4 oz grapefruit juice
- 1/2 oz lime juice
- 1/4 oz grenadine
- Dash of Angostura bitters
- Crushed ice
- Pineapple leaves, mint sprig, and edible orchid for garnish

Instructions:
1. In a blender, combine aged Jamaican rum, overproof rum, apricot liqueur, falernum, cinnamon syrup, grapefruit juice, lime juice, grenadine, and a dash of Angostura bitters.
2. Blend with a scoop of crushed ice until smooth.
3. Pour into a tiki mug or large glass filled with crushed ice.
4. Garnish with pineapple leaves, a mint sprig, and an edible orchid for a touch of extravagance.

Sip and savor the opulence of this Tiki Bar-style Elevated Zombie Punch, a lavish wist on the classic with high-quality ingredients and a stunning presentation.

THE
HERBS + SPICES

Savory Steakhouse Blend

Elevate your culinary experience with the epitome of taste luxury. Our Savory Steakhouse Blend boasts top-tier ingredients, including freshly ground black pepper, high-quality garlic powder, Spanish sweet smoked paprika, Himalayan pink salt, and dried French thyme. Delight in a more nuanced and sophisticated flavor profile, enhancing the richness of your steaks or burgers to a new level of gastronomic opulence.

Herb de Provence Infusion

Embark on a culinary journey to the heart of Provence with our Herb de Provence Infusion, an exquisite rendition of a timeless classic. This elevated blend is a testament to the pursuit of culinary excellence, featuring handpicked, region-specific herbs that transport your senses to the sun-kissed fields of Southern France.

Indulge in the fragrant embrace of dried thyme, preferably French thyme, interwoven with the nuanced richness of freshly crushed rosemary. Culinary lavender buds, a signature element, impart a delicate floral essence, while the Mediterranean marjoram and Greek oregano contribute their distinct Mediterranean charm.

Citrusy Lemon-Pepper Mix

Unveil a culinary masterpiece with our Citrusy Lemon-Pepper Mix (Affluent Edition), a symphony of flavors meticulously curated to elevate your gastronomic journey. Immerse your dishes in the brightness of organic lemon zest, intricately balanced with the robustness of freshly ground Tellicherry black peppercorns. The addition of dried and crushed Italian flat-leaf parsley brings a herbaceous elegance, while the subtlety of garlic granules adds depth.

To ensure a truly lavish experience, we've included the finest fleur de sel, amplifying the overall taste profile. This Citrusy Lemon-Pepper Mix (Affluent Edition) is your invitation to indulge in the pinnacle of flavor sophistication, turning every dish into a culinary masterpiece.

Smoky BBQ Rub

Ignite your barbecue experience with the Smoky BBQ Rub (Affluent Edition). Crafted with the finest ingredients, including Spanish smoked paprika (pimentón de la Vera), muscovado or gourmet brown sugar, Aomori, Japan granulated garlic, shallot powder, and freshly toasted and ground cumin. Elevate your grilling game with this luxurious blend, boasting a sophisticated and complex flavor profile for an unparalleled BBQ sensation.

THE
RECIPES

Savory Steakhouse Blend: Elevating Every Bite

Welcome to a culinary journey where each bite tells a story of refinement and flavor exploration. In this chapter, our focus revolves around the Savory Steakhouse Blend, a harmonious fusion of garlic, smoked paprika, black pepper, and dried thyme.

These meticulously crafted recipes are more than just a collection; they're a celebration of elevated dining, introducing exotic and unique twists to classic steakhouse dishes. From saffron-infused ribeye steaks to miso-ginger steak bites, each recipe is a testament to the art of transforming a meal into an extraordinary experience.

Join us as we embark on a gastronomic adventure, exploring the nuances of flavor that the Savory Steakhouse Blend brings to every dish, turning ordinary moments into extraordinary memories.

Saffron-Infused Ribeye Steaks

Ingredients:
- 2 ribeye steaks
- Pinch of saffron threads
- 2 tablespoons Savory Steakhouse Blend
- Salt and pepper to taste
- 2 tablespoons olive oil

Instructions:
1. Crush saffron threads and mix with Savory Steakhouse Blend, salt, and pepper.
2. Rub the spice blend evenly over both sides of the ribeye steaks.
3. Drizzle olive oil over the steaks, ensuring they are well-coated.
4. Allow the steaks to marinate for at least 30 minutes.
5. Preheat the grill or a skillet over medium-high heat.
6. Grill the steaks for 4-5 minutes per side for medium-rare, adjusting for preferred doneness.
7. Rest the steaks for a few minutes before slicing.
8. Serve the saffron-infused ribeye steaks with your favorite sides and enjoy the exotic and flavorful experience.

Savory Herb Filet Mignon

Ingredients:
- 2 filet mignon steaks
- 2 tablespoons Savory Steakhouse Blend
- Salt and pepper to taste
- 1 tablespoon olive oil

Instructions:
1. Preheat your oven to 400°F (200°C).
2. Rub Savory Steakhouse Blend, salt, and pepper over both sides of the filet mignon steaks.
3. Heat olive oil in an oven-safe skillet over medium-high heat.
4. Sear the steaks for 2-3 minutes on each side until a golden crust forms.
5. Transfer the skillet to the preheated oven and roast for 5-7 minutes for medium-rare.
6. Rest the steaks for a couple of minutes before serving.

Enjoy this quick and flavorful Savory Herb Filet Mignon for an elevated dining experience.

Chimichurri Steak Fajitas

Ingredients:
- 1 lb flank steak, thinly sliced
- 1 red bell pepper, thinly sliced
- 1 green bell pepper, thinly sliced
- 1 large onion, thinly sliced
- 1/4 cup fresh cilantro, chopped

For the Chimichurri:
- 1 cup fresh parsley, chopped
- 3 cloves garlic, minced
- 1/2 cup extra-virgin olive oil
- 2 tablespoons red wine vinegar
- 1 teaspoon Savory Steakhouse Blend
- Salt and pepper to taste

Instructions:
1. In a bowl, combine all chimichurri ingredients and set aside.
2. Season the sliced flank steak with Savory Steakhouse Blend and let it marinate for at least 15 minutes.
3. Heat a skillet over medium-high heat. Add the marinated steak and cook until browned and cooked to your liking.
4. Remove the steak from the skillet and set it aside.
5. In the same skillet, add a bit more oil if needed, and sauté the sliced bell peppers and onions until they are tender-crisp.
6. Return the cooked steak to the skillet, add chopped cilantro, and pour half of the chimichurri sauce over the mixture. Toss to combine.
7. Warm the tortillas and spoon the steak and vegetable mixture onto each tortilla.
8. Drizzle with extra chimichurri sauce before serving.

Enjoy these Chimichurri Steak Fajitas for a burst of savory and herbaceous flavors that elevate the classic fajita experience.

Miso-Ginger Steak Bites

Ingredients:
- 1 lb sirloin or flank steak, bite-sized pieces
- 2 tbsp white miso paste
- 1 tbsp fresh ginger, grated
- 2 tbsp soy sauce
- 1 tbsp sesame oil
- 1 tbsp honey
- 1 tsp Savory Steakhouse Blend
- 2 tbsp vegetable oil
- Sesame seeds and green onions for garnish

Instructions:
1. Whisk miso paste, ginger, soy sauce, sesame oil, honey, and Savory Steakhouse Blend for the marinade.
2. Marinate steak pieces for 30 minutes.
3. Sear in a hot skillet with vegetable oil for 2-3 minutes per side.
4. Garnish with sesame seeds and green onions.

Enjoy these Miso-Ginger Steak Bites, bursting with savory and aromatic flavors.

Harissa-Spiced Vegetable Skewers

Ingredients:
- Assorted vegetables (bell peppers, cherry tomatoes, zucchini, red onion)
- 2 tablespoons harissa paste
- 2 tablespoons olive oil
- 1 teaspoon Savory Steakhouse Blend
- Salt and pepper to taste
- Wooden skewers, soaked in water

Instructions:
1. Preheat the grill or grill pan.
2. In a bowl, mix harissa paste, olive oil, Savory Steakhouse Blend, salt, and pepper to create the marinade.
3. Thread the assorted vegetables onto the soaked skewers.
4. Brush the vegetable skewers generously with the harissa marinade.
5. Grill the skewers for 8-10 minutes, turning occasionally until the vegetables are charred and tender.
6. Serve the Harissa-Spiced Vegetable Skewers hot, offering a delightful blend of smoky, spicy, and savory flavors.

These vegetable skewers are a quick and vibrant dish, perfect for bringing a taste of North African cuisine to your table.

Gochujang Steakhouse Burgers

Ingredients:
- 1 lb ground beef
- 2 tbsp Gochujang
- 1 tbsp Savory Steakhouse Blend
- 1 tbsp soy sauce
- 1 tsp sesame oil
- 4 burger buns
- Lettuce, tomato, and toppings

Instructions:
1. Mix ground beef with Gochujang, Savory Steakhouse Blend, soy sauce, and sesame oil.
2. Shape into four patties and grill for 4-5 minutes per side.
3. Toast burger buns on the grill.
4. Assemble burgers with lettuce, tomato, and toppings.
5. Serve these Gochujang Steakhouse Burgers hot, marrying Korean spice with classic steakhouse flavor.

Soy-Wasabi Steak Kebabs

Ingredients:
- 1 lb sirloin steak, cubed
- 2 tbsp soy sauce
- 1 tbsp wasabi paste
- 1 tsp Savory Steakhouse Blend
- 1 tbsp sesame oil
- Wooden skewers

Instructions:
1. Mix soy sauce, wasabi paste, Savory Steakhouse Blend, and sesame oil.
2. Thread steak cubes onto skewers and brush with the marinade.
3. Grill for 8-10 minutes until cooked to your liking.
4. Serve these Soy-Wasabi Steak Kebabs hot, delivering a fusion of savory, spicy, and umami flavors.

Indulge in a burst of bold flavors with these succulent sirloin steak kebabs. Marinated in a blend of soy sauce, wasabi paste, and the rich Savory Steakhouse Blend, these kebabs promise a sizzling journey of savory, spicy, and umami goodness. Perfect for a quick and flavorful grilling experience.

Rosemary-Smoked Paprika Roast Beef

Ingredients:
- 2 lbs beef roast
- 2 tablespoons olive oil
- 1 tablespoon Savory Steakhouse Blend
- 1 tablespoon smoked paprika
- 1 tablespoon fresh rosemary, chopped
- Salt and pepper to taste

Instructions:
1. Preheat the oven to 375°F (190°C).
2. Rub the beef roast with olive oil, Savory Steakhouse Blend, smoked paprika, fresh rosemary, salt, and pepper.
3. Place the seasoned roast on a roasting pan.
4. Roast in the oven for about 25-30 minutes per pound or until the internal temperature reaches your preferred level of doneness.
5. Rest the roast for 10 minutes before slicing.

Indulge in the rich aroma and savory notes of this Rosemary-Smoked Paprika Roast Beef, a simple yet elegant dish perfect for any occasion.

Lemon-Basil Steak with a Twist

Ingredients:
- 1 lb sirloin or flank steak
- Zest of 1 lemon
- Juice of 1 lemon
- 2 tablespoons fresh basil, chopped
- 1 tablespoon Savory Steakhouse Blend
- 2 tablespoons honey (the twist)
- Salt and pepper to taste

Instructions:
1. Preheat the grill or stovetop griddle.
2. Zest and juice the lemon into a bowl, add chopped basil, Savory Steakhouse Blend, honey, salt, and pepper to create the marinade.
3. Coat the steak in the lemon-basil mixture, ensuring it's well-covered.
4. Grill the steak for 4-5 minutes per side or until it reaches your preferred level of doneness.
5. Let it rest for a few minutes before slicing.

Enjoy this Lemon-Basil Steak with an unexpected touch of honey, adding a delightful sweetness to the savory and citrusy flavors.

Green Peppercorn and Thyme Steak Skillet with a Guajillo Twist

Ingredients:
- 1 lb sirloin steak, thinly sliced
- 2 tablespoons green peppercorns
- 1 tablespoon fresh thyme leaves
- 1 tablespoon Savory Steakhouse Blend
- 1 tablespoon olive oil
- 1 dehydrated guajillo pepper, rehydrated and thinly sliced
- Salt and pepper to taste

Instructions:
1. Rehydrate the guajillo pepper by soaking it in hot water for 15-20 minutes, then thinly slice.
2. Heat olive oil in a skillet over medium-high heat.
3. Add sliced sirloin steak, green peppercorns, fresh thyme leaves, Savory Steakhouse Blend, and sauté until the steak is browned.
4. Toss in the rehydrated and sliced guajillo pepper, cook for an additional 2-3 minutes until it imparts its spicy flavor to the dish.
5. Season with salt and pepper to taste.
6. Serve this Green Peppercorn and Thyme Steak Skillet hot, enjoying the aromatic blend of herbs, spices, and the unique heat from the guajillo pepper.

This dish offers a spicy twist with the bold flavor of the rehydrated guajillo pepper, adding depth and complexity to the Green Peppercorn and Thyme Steak Skillet.

To substitute guajillo pepper powder for a whole guajillo pepper, you can generally use about 1 to 1.5 teaspoons of guajillo powder for each pepper. In this case, with one dehydrated guajillo pepper, you can start with 1 teaspoon of guajillo powder and adjust according to your taste preferences. Keep in mind that the heat level can vary, so it's advisable to start with a smaller amount and add more if needed.

Herb de Provence Infusion :
A Sophisticated Difference

This sophisticated blend of Provencal herbs is meticulously
curated for culinary excellence. Handpicked ingredients,
including French thyme, freshly crushed rosemary, culinary
lavender buds, Mediterranean marjoram, and Greek oregano,
create a symphony of flavors that transport your palate to the
sun-kissed fields of Southern France.

Potential Uses:

1. Classic Dishes: Elevate roast chicken, lamb, or beef with a
generous sprinkle of this infusion for a Provencal touch.

2. Vegetarian Delights: Enhance the flavor of roasted or grilled
vegetables, soups, and stews for a herbaceous and aromatic
experience.

3. Breads and Pastries: Add a pinch to bread dough, focaccia,
or savory pastries to infuse them with a Mediterranean flair.

4. Appetizers: Sprinkle over goat cheese, mix into dips, or use
as a finishing touch on bruschetta for an appetizer that bursts
with flavor.

5. Grilled Seafood: Transform grilled fish or seafood by
seasoning with this infusion, adding a layer of complexity to
your oceanic dishes.

Comparison to Other Blends:

1. Tuscan Herb Blend: While both blends feature
Mediterranean influences, Herb de Provence Infusion has a
more pronounced floral note due to the addition of lavender,
setting it apart from the earthier Tuscan blend.

2. Italian Seasoning: Herb de Provence Infusion is a step further with its specific Provencal herbs, offering a more complex and nuanced flavor compared to the simpler Italian seasoning.

3. Traditional Herbes de Provence: Our Mid-Century Edition distinguishes itself with its focus on premium ingredients, ensuring a heightened level of sophistication in taste and aroma.

In essence, Herb de Provence Infusion stands out as a premium blend that captures the essence of Provencal cuisine, offering a versatile and luxurious addition to a wide array of dishes. Choose the Herb de Provence Infusion for a mid-century modern dinner party to infuse classic dishes with a touch of Southern French sophistication, bringing a timeless yet elevated culinary experience to your guests.

Herbed Roast Chicken with Pineapple and Chili

Ingredients:
- 1 whole chicken (about 4-5 lbs)
- 2 tablespoons Herb de Provence Infusion
- 1 cup fresh pineapple juice
- 1 tablespoon chili flakes
- Salt and pepper to taste
- Olive oil

Instructions:
1. Preheat your oven to 375°F (190°C).
2. Rinse the chicken and pat it dry with paper towels. Place it in a roasting pan.
3. In a small bowl, mix Herb de Provence Infusion, fresh pineapple juice, chili flakes, salt, and pepper.
4. Brush the chicken with olive oil, ensuring it's evenly coated.
5. Pour the pineapple and chili mixture over the chicken, making sure to get it into all the nooks and crannies.
6. Roast in the preheated oven for about 1.5 to 2 hours or until the internal temperature reaches 165°F (74°C).
7. Baste the chicken with the pan juices every 30 minutes for a flavorful and moist result.
8. Once done, let the chicken rest for a few minutes before carving.

The Herbed Roast Chicken with Pineapple and Chili is an enticing choice for several reasons:

1. Balanced Fusion of Flavors: The Herb de Provence Infusion, with its blend of Provencal herbs, is a versatile base. Combining it with the sweetness of fresh pineapple juice and the heat from chili flakes creates a harmonious fusion of flavors.

2. Global Culinary Fusion: This recipe represents a culinary fusion that transcends traditional boundaries. It draws inspiration from both Provencal and tropical cuisines, resulting in a unique and exciting dish.

3. Contrasting Elements: The sweetness from pineapple provides a delightful contrast to the savory herbs, while the chili adds a hint of heat. This interplay of sweet, savory, and spicy elements makes the dish intriguing and memorable.

4. Adaptability: The Herb de Provence Infusion serves as a versatile and adaptable seasoning, making it an excellent choice for experimenting with various global flavors. It pairs exceptionally well with both traditional and exotic ingredients.

5. Ease of Preparation: Despite its sophisticated flavor profile, this recipe is straightforward to prepare. The infusion of flavors happens effortlessly during the roasting process, requiring minimal hands-on time.

6. Appealing Presentation: The resulting roast chicken is not only flavorful but also visually appealing. The caramelization of pineapple and herbs creates an enticing golden hue on the skin.

7. Versatile Occasion: This dish is suitable for various occasions, from family dinners to special gatherings. Its unique combination of flavors makes it a conversation starter and a crowd-pleaser.

In summary, the Herbed Roast Chicken with Pineapple and Chili offers a delightful blend of flavors, a touch of global inspiration, and an approachable yet gourmet appeal, making it a standout choice for those looking to elevate their roast chicken experience.

Crispy Chicken Skin Techniques

Achieving crispy skin on a roast chicken is a culinary delight. Here are some tricks to ensure you get that perfect, crispy finish:

1. Dry the Skin:
 - Before roasting, pat the chicken skin completely dry using paper towels. Moisture on the skin inhibits crispiness, so removing excess water is crucial.

2. Air Drying:
 - For an extra crispy result, let the chicken air dry in the refrigerator uncovered for a few hours or overnight. This helps to eliminate surface moisture.

3. Salt the Skin:
 - Rubbing salt onto the chicken skin helps draw out more moisture and enhances the crispiness. Season the skin generously with kosher or sea salt.

4. Use Baking Powder:
 - Mixing a small amount of baking powder with the salt can aid in achieving a crispier skin. Ensure it's thoroughly combined with the salt before applying.

5. High Initial Temperature:
 - Start the roasting process at a higher temperature, around 425°F (220°C), for the first 20-30 minutes. This initial blast of heat helps to quickly render the fat, contributing to crispy skin.

6. Butter or Oil Rub:
 - Rubbing the skin with softened butter or oil promotes browning and crispiness. You can even mix herbs or spices into the butter or oil for added flavor.

7. Elevate the Chicken:

- Use a roasting rack or vegetables under the chicken to elevate it. This allows hot air to circulate around the entire bird, promoting even crisping.

8. Flip or Turn the Chicken:

- If possible, flip the chicken onto its breast halfway through the roasting time. This helps the back side of the chicken to crisp up as well. Alternatively, you can turn the chicken during roasting.

9. Render the Fat:

- Ensure the chicken is properly trussed, and if it has excess fat in the cavity, consider removing it. This helps the skin to crisp up without being weighed down.

10. Finish with High Heat:

- Towards the end of the roasting time, increase the temperature to give the skin a final boost of heat. Keep an eye on it to prevent burning.

Remember to monitor the internal temperature of the chicken to ensure it's cooked through while achieving that coveted crispy skin.

Herbed Roast Chicken with Pistachio Dukkah

Ingredients:
- 1 whole chicken (about 4-5 lbs)
- 2 tablespoons Herb de Provence Infusion
- 1 cup shelled pistachios
- 2 tablespoons sesame seeds
- 1 tablespoon coriander seeds
- 1 tablespoon cumin seeds
- Salt and pepper to taste
- Olive oil

Instructions:
1. Preheat your oven to 375°F (190°C).
2. Rinse the chicken and pat it dry with paper towels. Place it in a roasting pan.
3. In a small bowl, mix Herb de Provence Infusion, salt, and pepper. Rub the mixture all over the chicken, ensuring even coverage.
4. In a dry skillet over medium heat, toast the pistachios, sesame seeds, coriander seeds, and cumin seeds until fragrant. Allow them to cool.
5. In a food processor, pulse the toasted ingredients until they form a coarse crumbly texture, creating the pistachio dukkah.
6. Brush the chicken with olive oil and sprinkle a generous layer of the pistachio dukkah over the top.
7. Roast in the preheated oven for about 1.5 to 2 hours or until the internal temperature reaches 165°F (74°C).
8. Once done, let the chicken rest for a few minutes before carving.

Elevate your culinary experience with this enticing Herbed Roast Chicken, infused with the sophisticated Herb de Provence Infusion and crowned with a flavorful Pistachio Dukkah crust.

Key Features:

- **Provencal Elegance:** The blend of Herb de Provence Infusion introduces a medley of French thyme, crushed rosemary, culinary lavender buds, Mediterranean marjoram, and Greek oregano, creating a Provencal-inspired flavor profile.

- **Nutty and Aromatic Dukkah:** The Pistachio Dukkah, a blend of toasted pistachios, sesame seeds, coriander seeds, and cumin seeds, imparts a nutty and aromatic crunch, adding depth and texture to the roast chicken.

- **Simple Preparation:** This recipe offers a straightforward preparation process, making it accessible for home cooks while delivering a gourmet dining experience.

- **Versatility:** The harmonious combination of Provencal herbs and nutty dukkah makes this roast chicken suitable for various occasions, from family dinners to special celebrations.

- **Visual Appeal:** The golden brown crust of pistachio dukkah creates an appealing visual contrast, making this dish not only delectable but also visually enticing.

Serve and Impress:

Present this Herbed Roast Chicken with Pistachio Dukkah as the centerpiece of your table, and let the delightful aroma and exquisite flavors captivate your guests. Perfect for those seeking a culinary journey that balances tradition with a touch of modern sophistication.

Lavender Honey Glazed Salmon

Ingredients:
- 4 salmon fillets
- 2 tablespoons Herb de Provence Infusion
- 1/4 cup honey (preferably lavender-infused)
- 2 tablespoons soy sauce
- 1 tablespoon olive oil
- Salt and pepper to taste
- Fresh lavender sprigs for garnish (optional)

Instructions:
1. Preheat your oven to 375°F (190°C) and line a baking sheet with parchment paper.
2. In a small bowl, mix the Herb de Provence Infusion, lavender-infused honey, soy sauce, olive oil, salt, and pepper.
3. Place the salmon fillets on the prepared baking sheet, skin-side down.
4. Brush the salmon fillets generously with the lavender honey mixture, ensuring they are well-coated.
5. Bake in the preheated oven for 12-15 minutes or until the salmon flakes easily with a fork.
6. For a caramelized finish, broil for an additional 2-3 minutes.
7. Remove from the oven, garnish with fresh lavender sprigs if desired, and serve.

Indulge in a culinary masterpiece with this Lavender Honey Glazed Salmon, a dish that seamlessly blends the Provencal elegance of Herb de Provence Infusion with the delicate sweetness of lavender-infused honey. The infusion of French thyme, crushed rosemary, culinary lavender buds, Mediterranean marjoram, and Greek oregano elevates the salmon to new heights, transporting your palate to the sun-drenched landscapes of Southern France. The honey glaze, enriched with the aromatic notes of lavender, creates a perfect harmony with the natural flavors of the salmon, resulting in a succulent and nuanced dish that is as visually stunning as it is delectable.

This recipe offers simplicity in preparation, making it accessible for both novice and seasoned cooks. The infusion process infuses the salmon with a rich herbaceous flavor, while the honey glaze, with its hint of lavender sweetness, provides a delightful balance. Whether for an intimate dinner or a special occasion, the Lavender Honey Glazed Salmon promises to be a captivating centerpiece, marrying the sophistication of Provencal cuisine with the allure of sweet, floral undertones for a truly memorable dining experience.

Lemon-Lavender Herbed Pasta with Herb de Provence Infusion

Ingredients:
- 8 oz pasta of your choice
- 2 tablespoons Herb de Provence Infusion
- Zest of 1 lemon
- 2 tablespoons fresh lemon juice
- 3 tablespoons olive oil
- 2 cloves garlic, minced
- 1 teaspoon dried culinary lavender buds
- Salt and pepper to taste
- Grated Parmesan cheese (optional)
- Fresh parsley for garnish

Instructions:
1. Cook the pasta according to the package instructions until al dente. Reserve 1/2 cup of pasta cooking water before draining.
2. In a large pan, heat olive oil over medium heat. Add minced garlic and sauté until fragrant.
3. Sprinkle Herb de Provence Infusion into the pan and stir to infuse the oil and garlic with the herbal blend.
4. Add lemon zest, lemon juice, and dried lavender buds to the pan. Stir to combine.
5. Toss the cooked pasta into the pan, ensuring it's well-coated with the infused oil and flavors. If the mixture seems dry, add a splash of the reserved pasta cooking water.
6. Season with salt and pepper to taste. For an extra layer of flavor, sprinkle with grated Parmesan cheese if desired.
7. Serve the Lemon-Lavender Herbed Pasta in individual plates, garnished with fresh parsley for a burst of color and freshness.

This simple yet exquisite dish seamlessly blends the vibrant citrusy notes of lemon, the aromatic essence of dried lavender buds, and the Provencal sophistication of the herbal infusion.

The flavors dance harmoniously with each twirl of pasta, coated in a luscious olive oil and garlic base.

This creation not only brings a touch of Southern French elegance to your table but also exemplifies the beauty of simplicity, allowing the herbaceous blend to shine alongside the bright zest of lemon and the delicate floral hints of lavender. Sprinkle with Parmesan and garnish with fresh parsley for an extra layer of indulgence, turning every bite into a culinary journey through the sun-kissed landscapes of Provence.

Grilled Herbed Vegetables with Feta

Ingredients:
- Assorted vegetables (zucchini, bell peppers, cherry tomatoes, red onions, etc.), sliced for grilling
- 2 tablespoons Herb de Provence Infusion
- 3 tablespoons olive oil
- Salt and pepper to taste
- 1/2 cup crumbled feta cheese
- Fresh herbs (such as parsley or basil) for garnish

Instructions:
1. Preheat the grill to medium-high heat.
2. In a large bowl, toss the sliced vegetables with Herb de Provence Infusion, olive oil, salt, and pepper until evenly coated.
3. Arrange the vegetables on the preheated grill grates. Grill for 8-10 minutes, turning occasionally, until they are tender and have a nice char.
4. Once the vegetables are grilled to perfection, transfer them to a serving platter.
5. Sprinkle crumbled feta cheese generously over the grilled vegetables while they are still warm, allowing it to slightly melt.
6. Garnish with fresh herbs for a burst of color and added freshness.
7. Serve these Grilled Herbed Vegetables with Feta as a delightful side dish or a standalone vegetarian option, showcasing the Provencal herb blend's aromatic charm and complemented by the creamy richness of feta.

The star of this dish is the Herb de Provence Infusion, which infuses the assortment of grilled vegetables with its Provencal charm. The aromatic blend of French thyme, crushed rosemary, culinary lavender buds, Mediterranean marjoram, and Greek oregano creates a herbaceous dance on the palate, perfectly complemented by the smoky char from the grill. As the vegetables reach a tender perfection, a generous sprinkle of crumbled feta adds a creamy and tangy contrast, marrying the richness of the cheese with the vibrant, grilled medley.

1. Mediterranean Twist: Introduce a Mediterranean flair by drizzling the grilled vegetables with balsamic glaze and adding Kalamata olives and diced cucumber. The sweet acidity of the balsamic and the briny olives will add depth to the dish.

2. Citrus Infusion: Before grilling, marinate the vegetables in a mixture of olive oil, Herb de Provence Infusion, and citrus juice (lemon or orange). After grilling, sprinkle with crumbled feta and fresh mint for a refreshing and citrusy twist on the classic recipe.

Citrusy Lemon-Pepper Mix:
A Revised Classic

Delight your senses with the zesty sophistication of the Citrusy Lemon-Pepper Mix, carefully curated in the Affluent Edition. This exquisite blend features a harmonious marriage of premium ingredients, including organic lemon zest, freshly ground Tellicherry black peppercorns, dried and crushed Italian flat-leaf parsley, garlic granules, and the luxurious touch of Fleur de sel. This blend captures the essence of a sunny citrus grove with a peppery kick, providing a burst of flavor that elevates your culinary creations.

Points of Distinction:

1. Premium Ingredients: The Mid-Century Dinner Party Edition prioritizes quality with the use of organic lemon zest, Tellicherry black peppercorns, and high-grade sea salt, ensuring a superior taste experience compared to standard lemon-pepper blends.

2. Balanced Citrusy and Peppery Notes: The blend strikes a perfect balance between the bright, citrusy profile from the lemon zest and the bold, peppery warmth from the Tellicherry black peppercorns, creating a versatile seasoning for a variety of dishes.

3. Enhanced with Sea Salt: The addition of Fleur de sel enhances the overall flavor profile, providing a nuanced saltiness that complements the citrus and pepper elements, making it a well-rounded seasoning.

Usage Suggestions:

1. Grilled Proteins: Sprinkle this Citrusy Lemon-Pepper Mix on grilled chicken, fish, or shrimp for a refreshing and peppery twist.

2. Vegetable Medley: Elevate roasted or grilled vegetables by tossing them with this blend before cooking to add a burst of citrusy and peppery goodness.

3. Pasta and Salads: Enhance the flavor of pasta dishes and salads by incorporating this blend into dressings or sprinkling it directly for a zesty kick.

4. Marinades: Create vibrant marinades for meats and seafood by combining this mix with olive oil, lemon juice, and herbs.

This Citrusy Lemon-Pepper Mix stands out as a superior seasoning, marrying premium ingredients to deliver a luxurious blend that enhances a wide range of culinary creations.

Lemon-Pepper Whipped Feta Dip

Ingredients:
- 8 oz feta cheese, crumbled
- 2 tablespoons Citrusy Lemon-Pepper Mix
- 1/4 cup Greek yogurt
- 2 tablespoons extra-virgin olive oil
- Fresh herbs (such as dill or chives) for garnish
- Crackers or sliced vegetables for serving

Instructions:
1. In a food processor, combine crumbled feta, Citrusy Lemon-Pepper Mix, Greek yogurt, and olive oil.
2. Blend until the mixture becomes smooth and creamy, scraping down the sides as needed.
3. Transfer the whipped feta dip to a serving bowl.
4. Garnish with fresh herbs and drizzle with a bit of extra olive oil.
5. Serve with your favorite crackers or a colorful array of sliced vegetables.

Immerse your taste buds in a burst of Mediterranean flavors with this Lemon-Pepper Whipped Feta Dip. The velvety smoothness of whipped feta meets the zesty notes of Citrusy Lemon-Pepper Mix, creating a dip that's both luxurious and refreshingly tangy. The Greek yogurt adds a hint of creaminess, while a drizzle of extra-virgin olive oil enhances the richness. Garnished with fresh herbs, this dip becomes a

captivating centerpiece for any gathering, embodying the essence of elevated simplicity.

Variation Ideas:

1. Sundried Tomato and Olive Whipped Feta Dip:
  Fold in chopped sundried tomatoes and Kalamata olives into

the whipped feta dip for a Mediterranean twist. The sun-drenched flavors pair perfectly with the citrusy brightness.

2. Honey and Thyme Infused Whipped Feta Dip:
Add a touch of sweetness by drizzling honey over the whipped feta dip and garnishing with fresh thyme leaves. This variation balances the savory and sweet notes, creating a delightful contrast.

3. Fig and Walnut Infused Whipped Feta Dip:
Incorporate the sweet and nutty flavors of dried figs and chopped walnuts into the whipped feta dip. Soak the figs in warm water until softened, then finely chop them. Fold both the figs and chopped walnuts into the whipped feta mixture. This variation adds a delightful contrast of textures and a hint of natural sweetness, making it a unique and delightful addition to your spread. Serve with artisanal whole grain crackers for an extra touch of sophistication.

Lemon-Pepper Buttered Lobster Tails

Ingredients:
- 4 lobster tails, split in half
- 1/2 cup unsalted butter, melted
- 2 tablespoons Citrusy Lemon-Pepper Mix
- 2 tablespoons fresh lemon juice
- Salt to taste
- Fresh parsley, chopped, for garnish

Instructions:
1. Preheat your oven broiler.
2. In a small bowl, mix melted butter, Citrusy Lemon-Pepper Mix, and fresh lemon juice.
3. Place the split lobster tails on a baking sheet, shell side down.
4. Brush the lobster meat generously with the lemon-pepper butter mixture.
5. Season with a pinch of salt to enhance the flavors.
6. Broil the lobster tails for about 8-10 minutes or until the lobster meat is opaque and slightly browned.
7. Remove from the oven and sprinkle chopped fresh parsley over the lobster tails for a burst of color and freshness.
8. Serve immediately, drizzling any remaining lemon-pepper butter over the lobster tails for extra flavor.

This rich and succulent lobster meat is bathed in a luscious blend of melted butter, Citrusy Lemon-Pepper Mix, and fresh lemon juice, creating a symphony of citrusy, peppery, and buttery notes. The lobster tails are delicately broiled to perfection, achieving a beautiful caramelization on the edges while ensuring the lobster meat remains tender and flavorful. Garnished with a sprinkle of fresh parsley, this dish not only tantalizes the taste buds but also captivates with its vibrant presentation. Perfect for a special dinner or any occasion where you want to indulge in the luxurious flavors of lobster enhanced with the bright essence of lemon and pepper.

Suggested Side:

Garlic Lemon-Pepper Roasted Asparagus:
 - Toss fresh asparagus spears in olive oil, minced garlic, and Citrusy Lemon-Pepper Mix.
 - Roast in the oven until the asparagus is tender yet still slightly crisp.
 - Squeeze fresh lemon juice over the roasted asparagus before serving. This side dish complements the lobster tails with its citrusy and garlicky notes.

Citrusy Couscous Salad:
 - Prepare a light and refreshing couscous salad with a citrusy twist. Combine cooked and cooled couscous with segments of grapefruit and orange. Add finely chopped mint, parsley, and a drizzle of lemon vinaigrette. The bright and zesty flavors of the salad will enhance the richness of the lobster tails.

Roasted Asparagus with Almond Gremolata:
 - Roast fresh asparagus spears until they're tender but still have a slight crunch. Create a vibrant almond gremolata by mixing finely chopped almonds, lemon zest, garlic, and parsley. Sprinkle the gremolata over the roasted asparagus just before serving. The combination of the nutty gremolata and the crisp-tender asparagus adds a delightful contrast to the succulent lobster.

These unexpected sides bring diverse textures and flavors to the plate, elevating your Lemon-Pepper Buttered Lobster Tails experience.

Lemon-Pepper Risotto

Ingredients:
- 1 cup Arborio rice
- 1/2 cup dry white wine
- 4 cups chicken or vegetable broth, kept warm
- 1/2 cup grated Parmesan cheese
- 2 tablespoons unsalted butter
- 1 tablespoon Citrusy Lemon-Pepper Mix
- Zest of one lemon
- Salt to taste
- Fresh parsley, chopped, for garnish

Instructions:
1. In a large pan, heat 1 tablespoon of butter over medium heat. Add Arborio rice and toast for 2-3 minutes until lightly golden.
2. Pour in the white wine, stirring constantly until the wine is mostly absorbed.
3. Begin adding warm broth one ladle at a time, allowing each addition to be absorbed before adding more. Continue stirring frequently.
4. When the rice is creamy and just tender (about 18-20 minutes), stir in the remaining tablespoon of butter, Parmesan cheese, Citrusy Lemon-Pepper Mix, lemon zest, and salt to taste.
5. Garnish with fresh parsley and serve warm. The bright citrusy notes of the lemon-pepper mix add a delightful twist to this classic Italian dish.

Lemon-Pepper Caesar Salad

Ingredients:
- Romaine lettuce, chopped
- Caesar dressing
- Croutons
- Parmesan cheese, shaved or grated
- Citrusy Lemon-Pepper Mix
- Lemon wedges for serving

Instructions:
1. In a large bowl, toss the chopped Romaine lettuce with Caesar dressing until evenly coated.
2. Sprinkle Citrusy Lemon-Pepper Mix over the salad, adjusting to your taste preference.
3. Add croutons and toss again to distribute evenly.
4. Top the salad with shaved or grated Parmesan cheese.
5. Serve immediately with lemon wedges on the side for an extra burst of citrus flavor. The Lemon-Pepper Caesar Salad is a refreshing and zesty companion to the richness of the lobster tails.

Citrusy Lemon-Pepper Grilled Shrimp Skewers

Ingredients:
- 1 pound large shrimp, peeled and deveined
- 2 tablespoons olive oil
- 2 tablespoons Citrusy Lemon-Pepper Mix
- 2 cloves garlic, minced
- Zest of one lemon
- Fresh parsley, chopped, for garnish
- Lemon wedges for serving

Instructions:
1. In a bowl, combine olive oil, Citrusy Lemon-Pepper Mix, minced garlic, and lemon zest.
2. Add the shrimp to the marinade, ensuring each shrimp is well-coated. Allow to marinate for at least 15 minutes.
3. Thread the marinated shrimp onto skewers.
4. Preheat the grill to medium-high heat.
5. Grill the shrimp skewers for 2-3 minutes per side or until they are opaque and have grill marks.
6. Remove from the grill and sprinkle with fresh parsley.
7. Serve the grilled shrimp skewers with lemon wedges for an extra squeeze of citrus.

These succulent shrimp are marinated in a vibrant blend of olive oil, Citrusy Lemon-Pepper Mix, garlic, and lemon zest, infusing them with a zesty and peppery kick. As they sizzle on the grill, the aroma of citrus and pepper will tantalize your senses. Garnished with fresh parsley, these skewers are a burst of freshness that pairs perfectly with the smoky char from the grill. Serve with lemon wedges for an additional bright touch.

Variation Ideas:

1. Citrusy Lemon-Pepper Shrimp Tacos:
   - Serve the grilled shrimp in warm tortillas with shredded cabbage, avocado slices, and a drizzle of citrusy aioli.

2. Lemon-Pepper Shrimp and Pineapple Skewers:
   - Alternate shrimp with pineapple chunks on the skewers for a sweet and savory tropical twist.

3. Citrusy Lemon-Pepper Shrimp Pasta:
   - Toss the grilled shrimp with cooked pasta, cherry tomatoes, and a light lemon-pepper vinaigrette for a refreshing pasta salad.

Complement the vibrant flavors of Citrusy Lemon-Pepper Grilled Shrimp Skewers with these three unexpected and delicious side dishes:

1. Mango Avocado Salsa:
   - Create a refreshing and tropical salsa by combining diced ripe mango, creamy avocado chunks, finely chopped red onion, cilantro, and a squeeze of lime juice. The sweet and tangy salsa adds a burst of freshness that pairs beautifully with the citrusy shrimp skewers.

2. Quinoa and Roasted Vegetable Salad:
   - Prepare a nutritious quinoa salad with roasted vegetables. Toss cooked quinoa with a medley of roasted cherry tomatoes, bell peppers, zucchini, and red onion. Drizzle with a lemony vinaigrette and garnish with fresh basil or mint. The quinoa salad provides a hearty and flavorful side to balance the lightness of the shrimp.

3. Crispy Parmesan Polenta Fries:
   - Cut polenta into fries, coat them with grated Parmesan, and bake until golden and crispy. Serve these savory polenta fries with a lemon aioli dipping sauce. The crispy exterior and creamy interior of the polenta fries offer a delightful contrast to the succulent grilled shrimp.

These unexpected sides add variety and depth to your meal, creating a memorable dining experience with Citrusy Lemon-Pepper Grilled Shrimp Skewers at the center.

Smoky BBQ Rub:
A Premium Selection

Indulge in the epitome of barbecue sophistication with our Smoky BBQ Rub (Affluent Edition). Crafted with the utmost care, this blend features Spanish smoked paprika (pimentón de la Vera), renowned for its intense smokiness and rich flavor. Complemented by the depth of Muscovado sugar or gourmet brown sugar, this rub achieves a perfect balance between sweet and savory.

The inclusion of granulated garlic from Aomori, Japan, adds a layer of complexity with its nuanced and robust garlic notes. Shallot powder elevates the aromatic profile, providing a subtle yet distinctive onion essence. Ground cumin, preferably freshly toasted and ground, ties the elements together with warm and earthy undertones.

Versatility:

This Smoky BBQ Rub transcends the ordinary, making it a versatile companion for various culinary creations. Whether coating ribs, brisket, or chicken before slow-smoking or grilling, this rub imparts a sophisticated smokiness that elevates your barbecue experience. It effortlessly transforms into a flavor enhancer for roasted vegetables, adding a gourmet touch to your side dishes.

Comparison:

What sets this rub apart is the meticulous selection of high-quality smoked paprika and premium spices. The use of Muscovado sugar adds depth, imparting a caramelized sweetness that complements the smoky notes. The marriage of Aomori garlic and shallot powder introduces a refined aromatic profile rarely found in traditional BBQ rubs. Elevate your barbecue mastery with this Affluent Edition, setting a new standard for sophistication and complexity in the realm of BBQ seasonings.

This rub transcends ordinary expectations, becoming a versatile companion in grilling and smoking as a dry rub, a base for meat marinades, or a seasoning for grilled vegetables, popcorn, homemade butters and vinegars.

Here are two glaze, one sauce (slop), and one vinegar idea to enhance dishes with the smoky goodness of Smoky BBQ Rub:

1. Maple-Bourbon Glaze:
  - Combine maple syrup, bourbon, a dash of Dijon mustard, and a generous amount of Smoky BBQ Rub in a saucepan. Simmer and reduce the mixture until it thickens into a glossy glaze. Brush this irresistible glaze over grilled chicken, pork, or even roasted vegetables for a sweet and smoky finish.

2. Honey-Chipotle Glaze:
  - Mix honey, finely minced chipotle peppers in adobo sauce, a squeeze of lime juice, and Smoky BBQ Rub. Heat the mixture until well combined. This glaze adds a perfect balance of sweet, smoky, and spicy notes. Brush it over grilled shrimp, ribs, or use it as a finishing glaze for smoked meats.

3. Bourbon-Infused BBQ Sloppy Joe Sauce:
  - Brown ground beef or plant-based alternative and add a mixture of ketchup, Worcestershire sauce, apple cider vinegar, brown sugar, and a generous amount of Smoky BBQ Rub. Amp up the flavor by adding a splash of bourbon. Simmer until the sauce thickens and coats the meat. Serve this savory, smoky Sloppy Joe mix on buns for a satisfying meal.

4. Smoky Balsamic Vinegar Reduction:
  - Create a smoky balsamic reduction by combining balsamic vinegar, a touch of honey, and Smoky BBQ Rub in a saucepan. Simmer until the mixture reduces to a thick, syrupy consistency. Drizzle this flavorful reduction over grilled steak, roasted vegetables, or even as a finishing touch to a Caprese salad for a unique twist.

Grilled Pineapple with BBQ Glaze

Ingredients:
- 1 ripe pineapple, peeled, cored, and sliced into rings
- 1/4 cup Smoky BBQ Rub (Affluent Edition)
- 2 tablespoons honey
- 1 tablespoon lime juice
- Fresh mint leaves for garnish (optional)

Instructions:
1. Preheat the grill to medium-high heat.
2. In a small bowl, combine Smoky BBQ Rub, honey, and lime juice. Stir well to create the BBQ glaze.
3. Brush the pineapple slices generously with the BBQ glaze on both sides.
4. Place the glazed pineapple slices directly on the preheated grill grates.
5. Grill for 2-3 minutes per side, or until grill marks appear, and the pineapple caramelizes slightly.
6. Remove the grilled pineapple from the heat and arrange on a serving platter.
7. Drizzle any remaining BBQ glaze over the top and garnish with fresh mint leaves if desired.

Indulge in the extraordinary with our Grilled Pineapple with BBQ Glaze, a culinary masterpiece that harmonizes the tropical sweetness of ripe pineapple with the sophisticated smokiness of our Smoky BBQ Rub (Affluent Edition). The pineapple rings, brushed with a luscious glaze made from the rub, honey, and lime juice, undergo a sizzling transformation on the grill. Witness the magic unfold as the pineapple caramelizes, creating a harmonious blend of sweet and smoky flavors. Each succulent bite is a journey through tropical paradise, elevated by the complexity of the BBQ glaze. This dish is not merely grilled pineapple; it's a symphony of flavors that captivates the palate with every mouthful. Serve it as a show-stopping dessert or a delightful side dish at your next barbecue gathering, and let the extraordinary become the standard.

Here's a creative variation combining Grilled Pineapple with BBQ Glaze and fried rice:

Grilled Pineapple BBQ Glazed Fried Rice

Ingredients:
- 1 cup cooked jasmine or basmati rice (preferably chilled)
- 1 cup pineapple chunks, grilled with BBQ glaze
- 1/2 cup diced bell peppers (assorted colors)
- 1/2 cup diced red onion
- 1/2 cup frozen peas and carrots, thawed
- 2 cloves garlic, minced
- 2 tablespoons soy sauce
- 1 tablespoon BBQ glaze (reserved from the grilled pineapple)
- 1 tablespoon vegetable oil
- Salt and pepper to taste
- Chopped green onions and cilantro for garnish

Instructions:
1. Preheat a Wok or Large Skillet:
   - Heat the vegetable oil in a wok or large skillet over medium-high heat.
2. Sauté Vegetables:
   - Add diced red onion, bell peppers, and garlic to the pan. Sauté until the vegetables are tender-crisp.
3. Add Peas and Carrots:
   - Toss in the thawed peas and carrots, continuing to cook for another 2-3 minutes.
4. Stir in Rice:
   - Add the chilled cooked rice to the pan. Break up any clumps and stir-fry to incorporate the vegetables evenly.
5. Soy Sauce and BBQ Glaze:
   - Drizzle soy sauce and the reserved BBQ glaze (from the

grilled pineapple) over the rice. Mix well to coat the rice evenly.

6. Grilled Pineapple:

   - Gently fold in the grilled pineapple chunks. Allow them to heat through in the fried rice.

7. Season and Garnish:

   - Season with salt and pepper to taste. Garnish with chopped green onions and cilantro for a burst of freshness.

8. Serve Hot:

   - Serve the Grilled Pineapple BBQ Glazed Fried Rice as a flavorful and unique side dish or enjoy it on its own.

This fusion dish brings together the smoky sweetness of grilled pineapple with the savory notes of BBQ glaze, creating a delightful twist on classic fried rice.

Suggested Sides:

Coconut-Lime Rice:
Elevate your pineapple with Coconut-Lime Rice, a simple yet vibrant side dish. Fragrant jasmine rice is cooked in a blend of creamy coconut milk and water, infused with the zesty essence of lime. The result is a light and refreshing accompaniment with a hint of tropical flair. Perfectly paired with grilled dishes, this Coconut-Lime Rice adds a delightful burst of flavor to your plate.

Ingredients:
- 1 cup jasmine rice
- 1 cup coconut milk
- 1 cup water
- Zest and juice of 1 lime
- Salt to taste
- Fresh cilantro for garnish

Instructions:
1. Rinse rice under cold water until clear.
2. In a saucepan, combine rice, coconut milk, water, lime zest,

and a pinch of salt.

3. Bring to a boil, then simmer covered for 15-20 minutes until rice is cooked.

4. Fluff with a fork, squeeze lime juice over, and garnish with fresh cilantro.

Chili-Lime Grilled Corn on the Cob:

Enhance your barbecue experience with Chili-Lime Grilled Corn on the Cob. This side dish takes sweet corn to the next level with a zesty and slightly spicy flavor profile. The chili-lime mixture, featuring the boldness of chili powder and the brightness of lime, infuses the corn with a delightful kick. Grilled to perfection, the corn develops a smoky char that complements the sweetness of the kernels. Garnished with fresh cilantro, this side dish is a symphony of flavors that beautifully complements the Grilled Pineapple with BBQ Glaze, creating a well-rounded and memorable meal.

Ingredients:
- 4 ears of corn, husked
- 2 tablespoons olive oil
- 1 teaspoon chili powder
- Zest and juice of 1 lime
- Salt and pepper to taste
- Fresh cilantro, chopped, for garnish

Instructions:
1. Preheat the grill to medium-high heat.

2. In a small bowl, mix together olive oil, chili powder, lime zest, lime juice, salt, and pepper.

3. Brush the corn with the chili-lime mixture, ensuring it's evenly coated.

4. Grill the corn for 10-15 minutes, turning occasionally, until charred and cooked through.

5. Remove from the grill, sprinkle with chopped cilantro, and serve.

Coffee-Smoked BBQ Ribs

Ingredients:
- 2 racks of baby back ribs
- 1/4 cup Smoky BBQ Rub
- 2 tablespoons finely ground coffee
- 2 tablespoons brown sugar
- 1 tablespoon paprika
- 1 tablespoon garlic powder
- 1 tablespoon onion powder
- 1 teaspoon cayenne pepper
- Salt and black pepper to taste
- 1 cup strong brewed coffee, cooled
- 1/2 cup apple cider vinegar
- BBQ sauce for glazing (optional)

Instructions:
1. Preheat your smoker to 225°F (107°C).
2. In a bowl, mix Smoky BBQ Rub, ground coffee, brown sugar, paprika, garlic powder, onion powder, cayenne pepper, salt, and black pepper to create the coffee-smoked rub.
3. Remove the membrane from the back of the ribs and rub the coffee-smoked rub generously over both sides.
4. In a spray bottle, combine brewed coffee and apple cider vinegar.
5. Place the ribs on the smoker grate and smoke for 4-5 hours, spraying with the coffee-vinegar mixture every hour to keep them moist.
6. Check for tenderness using the bend test or a meat thermometer. Ribs should reach an internal temperature of 190-203°F (88-95°C).
7. Optionally, glaze the ribs with your favorite BBQ sauce during the last 30 minutes of cooking.
8. Remove from the smoker, let them rest for 10 minutes, then slice and serve.

Dive into a realm of unparalleled flavor with our Coffee-Smoked BBQ Ribs, a culinary masterpiece that marries the robust smokiness of our Smoky BBQ Rub with the rich essence of finely ground coffee. The ribs, expertly coated in a coffee-smoked rub, embark on a journey in the smoker, absorbing layers of complexity and tenderness over several hours. As they smoke to perfection, a symphony of aromas fills the air, showcasing the deep, earthy notes of coffee intertwined with the sophisticated flavors of the BBQ rub. The result is nothing short of extraordinary – tender, flavorful ribs that stand as a testament to the artistry of barbecue. Elevate your grilling experience with these Coffee-Smoked BBQ Ribs, where every bite unveils a sensory adventure, inviting you to savor the intricate fusion of smokiness, spice, and the bold richness of coffee.

Smoky BBQ Rub Crusted Lamb Chops with Cherry Bourbon Reduction

Ingredients:
- 4 lamb chops, frenched
- 1/4 cup Smoky BBQ Rub (Affluent Edition)
- Salt and black pepper to taste
- 1/2 cup cherry preserves
- 1/4 cup bourbon

Instructions:
1. Preheat the grill to medium-high heat.
2. Season lamb chops with salt and black pepper.
3. Coat each chop generously with Smoky BBQ Rub, ensuring an even crust.
4. In a saucepan, heat cherry preserves and bourbon until it forms a thick reduction.
5. Grill the lamb chops, brushing them with the cherry bourbon reduction during the last few minutes of grilling.
6. Sprinkle a little extra Smoky BBQ Rub over the glazed chops.
7. Continue grilling until the lamb chops reach your desired level of doneness.
8. Remove from the grill, let them rest for a few minutes, and serve with a drizzle of the remaining cherry bourbon reduction.

Savor the sophistication of our Smoky BBQ Rub Crusted Lamb Chops with Cherry Bourbon Reduction. This simple yet luxurious recipe begins with perfectly seasoned lamb chops generously crusted with our Affluent Edition Smoky BBQ Rub. The real magic happens as the chops meet the grill, creating a caramelized, smoky exterior.

The pièce de résistance is the decadent Cherry Bourbon Reduction, adding a luscious sweetness with a hint of bourbon richness. Each bite is a symphony of flavors – the savory notes of the BBQ rub complemented by the fruity elegance of the cherry bourbon reduction. Elevate your dining experience with this gourmet dish, where simplicity meets sublime sophistication.

BBQ Rub Seasoned Sweet Potato Fries

Ingredients:
- 2 large sweet potatoes, cut into fries
- 2 tablespoons olive oil
- 2 tablespoons Smoky BBQ Rub (Affluent Edition)
- Salt to taste

Instructions:
1. Preheat the oven to 425°F (220°C).
2. In a bowl, toss sweet potato fries with olive oil until evenly coated.
3. Sprinkle Smoky BBQ Rub over the fries, ensuring they are well-seasoned.
4. Spread the seasoned sweet potato fries on a baking sheet in a single layer.
5. Bake for 20-25 minutes, turning halfway through, until the fries are golden and crispy.
6. Season with a pinch of salt immediately after removing from the oven.

Elevate your side game with these BBQ Rub Seasoned Sweet Potato Fries – a simple yet irresistible accompaniment to any meal. The natural sweetness of the sweet potatoes meets the bold and smoky notes of our Affluent Edition Smoky BBQ Rub, creating a harmonious blend of flavors. These fries are oven-baked to a crispy perfection, making them an easy and delightful addition to your barbecue feast.

BBQ Rub Marinated Portobello Mushrooms

Ingredients:
- 4 large portobello mushrooms, stems removed
- 1/4 cup olive oil
- 2 tablespoons Smoky BBQ Rub (Affluent Edition)
- Salt and black pepper to taste
- 2 cloves garlic, minced (optional)

Instructions:
1. Clean the portobello mushrooms with a damp cloth and pat them dry.
2. In a bowl, whisk together olive oil, Smoky BBQ Rub, salt, black pepper, and minced garlic.
3. Place the mushrooms in a shallow dish and brush both sides with the BBQ rub marinade, ensuring they are well-coated.
4. Let the mushrooms marinate for at least 30 minutes to allow the flavors to infuse.
5. Grill the portobello mushrooms for 5-7 minutes per side or until they are tender and have grill marks.
6. Serve the mushrooms as a side dish or as a main course.

Variation 1: BBQ Mushroom Burger

- Place the grilled portobello mushrooms on a bun, add your favorite burger toppings, and enjoy a delicious BBQ Mushroom Burger.

Variation 2: BBQ Mushroom Skewers

- Cut the marinated mushrooms into smaller pieces and thread them onto skewers. Grill the skewers for a few minutes on each side for a delightful BBQ Mushroom Skewer appetizer.

Transform your portobello mushrooms into a savory delight with our BBQ Rub marinade. This simple recipe infuses the meaty mushrooms with the rich and smoky flavors of the Affluent Edition Smoky BBQ Rub.

Smoky BBQ Rub Infused Whiskey Cocktail

Ingredients:
- 2 oz bourbon whiskey
- 1/2 oz simple syrup
- 1/4 oz fresh lemon juice
- 1/4 oz Smoky BBQ Rub (Affluent Edition)
- Ice cubes
- Lemon twist for garnish

Instructions:
1. In a shaker, combine bourbon whiskey, simple syrup, fresh lemon juice, and Smoky BBQ Rub.
2. Add ice cubes to the shaker and shake well.
3. Strain the mixture into a glass filled with ice.
4. Garnish with a twist of lemon.

Indulge in the rich and smoky notes of our Smoky BBQ Rub with this Infused Whiskey Cocktail. The bold flavors of the Affluent Edition BBQ Rub meld seamlessly with the warmth of bourbon, creating a sophisticated and savory libation. This cocktail is a celebration of complexity, where the smokiness of the rub adds a unique twist to the classic whiskey drink. Sip and savor the harmonious marriage of flavors in every nuanced drop.

Smoky BBQ Rub Crusted Salmon Fillets

Ingredients:
- 4 salmon fillets
- 2 tablespoons Smoky BBQ Rub (Affluent Edition)
- 1 tablespoon olive oil
- Salt and black pepper to taste
- Lemon wedges for serving

Instructions:
1. Preheat the oven to 400°F (200°C).
2. Pat the salmon fillets dry and brush them with olive oil.
3. Sprinkle Smoky BBQ Rub over the fillets, ensuring they are well-coated.
4. Season with salt and black pepper to taste.
5. Place the fillets on a baking sheet lined with parchment paper.
6. Bake for 12-15 minutes or until the salmon flakes easily with a fork.
7. Serve with lemon wedges on the side.

Elevate your salmon experience with our Smoky BBQ Rub Crusted Salmon Fillets. The Affluent Edition BBQ Rub adds a layer of smoky sophistication to perfectly baked salmon. The result is a dish that tantalizes the taste buds with a harmonious blend of savory, smoky, and subtly sweet flavors. Each bite is a journey into gourmet excellence, showcasing the versatility of our premium Smoky BBQ Rub.

BBQ Rub Spiced Dark Chocolate Truffles

Ingredients:
- 8 oz dark chocolate, finely chopped
- 1/2 cup heavy cream
- 2 tablespoons unsalted butter
- 1 tablespoon Smoky BBQ Rub (Affluent Edition)
- Cocoa powder for dusting (optional)

Instructions:
1. In a heatproof bowl, place the chopped dark chocolate.
2. In a small saucepan, heat the heavy cream and butter over medium heat until it just starts to simmer.
3. Pour the hot cream and butter mixture over the chopped chocolate. Let it sit for a minute to melt the chocolate.
4. Stir the mixture until smooth and well combined.
5. Add Smoky BBQ Rub to the chocolate ganache and mix thoroughly.
6. Cover the bowl and refrigerate the mixture for at least 2 hours or until it's firm enough to handle.
7. Using a melon baller or spoon, scoop out portions of the mixture and roll them into small truffle-sized balls.
8. Optional: Dust the truffles with cocoa powder for an extra layer of flavor.
9. Place the truffles on a parchment-lined tray and refrigerate for another 30 minutes before serving.

And, we end with our recipe for BBQ Rub Spiced Dark Chocolate Truffles. The rich and decadent dark chocolate ganache is infused with the savory and smoky notes of our Affluent Edition Smoky BBQ Rub, creating a unique and indulgent treat. These truffles are a delightful blend of sweetness and sophistication, making them a perfect after-dinner indulgence or a gourmet gift for chocolate lovers. The unexpected twist of BBQ rub adds a layer of complexity that elevates the classic chocolate truffle to a whole new level of culinary delight.

THE CONTEMPORARY PARTY

Revisiting the mid-century modern format, incorporating elevated and rare spice blends, reinventing cocktails, and creating a small gift book with innovative recipes can offer a unique and compelling experience for several reasons:

1. Nostalgia with a Modern Twist:

- People often feel nostalgic for the elegance and sophistication associated with mid-century modern aesthetics. By revisiting this format, you tap into a sense of nostalgia while infusing it with contemporary creativity.

2. Unique Culinary Experiences:

- Elevating and reinventing mid-century recipes with rare spice blends introduces a novel culinary experience. It provides an opportunity for individuals to explore and savor flavors that may not have been prevalent in the mid-20th century.

3. Artisanal and Rare Ingredients:

- Incorporating rare spice blends adds an element of exclusivity and uniqueness to the culinary offerings. Artisanal, hard-to-find ingredients can elevate the dining experience, making it special and memorable.

4. Cocktail Revival:

- The mid-century was known for its cocktail culture. Re-imagining classic cocktails and introducing new, innovative ones can capture the essence of that era while catering to contemporary tastes. It adds a touch of sophistication and novelty to social gatherings.

5. Creative Expression:

- Acquiring a small gift book with easy yet innovative recipes allows for creative expression. It's an opportunity to showcase culinary expertise, share personal twists on classic recipes, and present a curated collection of dishes that are both accessible and impressive.

6. Aesthetic Appeal:
  - The mid-century modern aesthetic is known for its clean lines, bold colors, and timeless appeal. Incorporating this aesthetic into the presentation of the gift book and culinary creations adds visual charm and sophistication.

7. Unique Gifting Experience:
  - A small gift book with curated recipes, paired with rare spice blends, becomes a unique and thoughtful gift. It offers recipients the chance to recreate sophisticated meals and cocktails at home, creating a memorable experience.

8. Culinary Exploration:
  - The curated collection encourages individuals to explore new flavors and cooking techniques. It provides an avenue for culinary enthusiasts to expand their palate and try their hand at creating dishes that blend tradition with innovation.

9. Social Connection:
  - Sharing a meal, whether in person or virtually, has a social dimension. The gift book and its associated culinary creations become a way to connect with others, fostering a sense of community and shared experiences.

In summary, revisiting the mid-century modern format, infusing it with rare spice blends, and creating a gift book with innovative recipes offers a fresh and exciting culinary journey that combines nostalgia with modern creativity. It appeals to those seeking unique, sophisticated, and memorable experiences in both cooking and entertaining.

THE ORIGINS OF THE PARTY

Mid-century modern cuisine and the concept of the dinner party are deeply rooted in the cultural and social changes that occurred in the mid-20th century, particularly in the United States. Here's an overview:

Mid-Century Modern Cuisine:

1. Post-War Prosperity: After World War II, the United States experienced a period of economic growth and prosperity. This led to changes in lifestyle, including a focus on leisure and entertainment.

2. Technological Advancements: The post-war era saw advancements in kitchen technology, with the rise of electric appliances and modern conveniences. This influenced cooking styles and allowed for more experimental and diverse dishes.

3. Influence of Television: The popularity of television, especially cooking shows, brought new culinary ideas into American homes. Figures like Julia Child and James Beard played significant roles in shaping mid-century modern cooking.

4. International Influences: Increased global communication and travel brought a more diverse range of ingredients and cooking techniques into American kitchens. This era witnessed a growing interest in international cuisines.

The Idea of the Dinner Party:

1. Social Changes: The 1950s and 1960s marked a period of social change. The dinner party became a way for people to showcase their social status, hospitality, and culinary skills.

2. Suburban Living: The post-war era saw a surge in suburban living. Homes with spacious dining areas became common, providing the perfect setting for hosting gatherings.

3. Cocktail Culture: The mid-century was known for its cocktail culture. Classic cocktails and the art of mixology became integral to dinner parties, with hosts showcasing their bar skills.

4. Entertaining at Home: With the rise of television and suburban lifestyles, entertaining at home became more popular. Dinner parties were an opportunity for people to come together, share good food, and enjoy each other's company.

5. Formal and Informal Gatherings: Depending on the occasion, dinner parties could be formal or informal. Formal dinners might involve elaborate table settings, multi-course meals, and fine china. Informal gatherings might focus on casual, family-style dining.

Overall, mid-century modern cuisine and dinner parties encapsulated a shift in how people approached food, entertaining, and socializing. The emphasis was on innovation, experimentation, and creating memorable experiences within the comfort of one's home.

PERSONALIZING THE FLAVOURS

Creating your own recipes based on the four spice blends while only having information about the ingredients and not the exact proportions can be a creative and rewarding process. Here's a step-by-step guide on how you can approach this:

Steps to Develop Your Own Recipes:

1. Understand the Flavor Profiles:
   - Begin by familiarizing yourself with the flavor profiles of each spice blend. Understand the dominant and subtle notes each ingredient contributes.

2. Experiment in Small Batches:
   - Start with small batches to experiment with the spice blends. Use them in various dishes and note the impact on flavor. Begin by adding a small amount and adjust based on taste.

3. Select Compatible Ingredients:
   - Choose ingredients that complement the flavors of the spice blends. Consider proteins, vegetables, grains, and other components that will work well with the unique characteristics of each blend.

4. Balance Flavors:
   - Aim for a balance of flavors – sweet, savory, spicy, and umami. Consider the intensity of each spice blend and balance them with other ingredients to create a harmonious taste.

5. Record Your Experiments:
   - Keep a record of the ingredients and proportions you use in each experiment. Note the adjustments you make and the resulting flavor profile. This will help you refine your recipes.

6. Pairing with Cooking Techniques:
   - Explore different cooking techniques such as grilling,

roasting, sautéing, or slow cooking. The cooking method can enhance or mellow the flavors of the spice blends.

7. Test Across Different Dishes:
  - Test the spice blends across a variety of dishes – from main courses to sides and even desserts. This will give you a broader understanding of the versatility of each blend.

8. Seek Feedback:
  - Share your creations with friends, family, or a taste-testing group. Collect feedback to understand how others perceive the flavors and whether any adjustments are needed.

§

Regarding Proportions:

1. Analyzing Ingredient Lists:
  - Study the ingredient lists for each spice blend. While it won't give you exact proportions, it can offer insights into the key ingredients and their order of prominence.

2. Start with Dominant Ingredients:
  - Begin by focusing on the dominant ingredients listed. These are likely to contribute the most to the overall flavor. Experiment with these ingredients in higher proportions initially.

3. Experiment and Adjust:
  - Use your palate as a guide. Start with small amounts of each ingredient, focusing on the dominant ones, and adjust based on taste. This process may involve several iterations.

4. Research Similar Blends:
  - Explore existing recipes or blends that are similar to the ones you want to create. While not identical, these recipes can provide insights into ingredient proportions.

5. Trust Your Taste Buds:
- Ultimately, trust your taste buds. Your preferences and the preferences of those you cook for will guide you in finding the right balance.

Purchase or Make Your Own Blends:

1. Purchase Pre-made Blends:
- If you prefer a shortcut or want to taste the exact blends before creating your recipes, you can purchase pre-made blends. This allows you to understand the intended flavor profile.

2. Experiment with Homemade Blends:
- Alternatively, if you enjoy the process of experimentation, try making your own small batches of each spice blend. This way, you have full control over the proportions and can tailor them to your preferences.

In summary, developing your own recipes based on the spice blends involves a combination of experimentation, understanding flavor profiles, and trusting your taste buds. Whether you choose to purchase pre-made blends or make your own, the key is to enjoy the creative process and craft dishes that resonate with your unique culinary vision.

HOSTING THE PERFECT PARTY

Throwing a successful dinner party with a mid-century modern theme involves a combination of thoughtful planning, attention to detail, and a nod to the distinctive elements of the mid-20th century. Here are the essential elements to consider:

1. Invitations:
- Design invitations that reflect the mid-century modern aesthetic. Consider bold colors, clean lines, and iconic mid-century design elements. Digital or printed invitations can set the tone for the event.

2. Setting the Scene:
- Choose a venue or decorate your home with mid-century modern furniture and decor. Incorporate iconic elements like Eames chairs, sleek sideboards, and geometric patterns. Create a cohesive color palette that reflects the era.

3. Table Setting:
- Opt for mid-century modern tableware, flatware, and glassware. Consider vintage pieces or modern items with a retro flair. Use bold, contrasting colors and geometric patterns for tablecloths and napkins.

4. Cocktail Hour:
- Set up a stylish cocktail bar featuring classic mid-century cocktails. Consider drinks like Martinis, Old Fashioneds, or Moscow Mules. Use vintage glassware and garnishes that were popular during the era.

5. Attire:
- Encourage guests to dress in mid-century modern-inspired attire. Think cocktail dresses, suits, and accessories that were fashionable in the 1950s and 1960s.

6. Music:
  - Curate a playlist with music from the mid-century era. Jazz, swing, and classic rock tunes can enhance the ambiance. Consider iconic artists like Frank Sinatra, Ella Fitzgerald, or Elvis Presley.

7. Menu:
  - Craft a menu inspired by mid-century cuisine but with a modern twist. Include classic dishes from the era such as Beef Wellington, Chicken a la King, or Jell-O salads. Incorporate fresh, high-quality ingredients to elevate the flavors.

8. Signature Drinks:
  - Create signature cocktails for the evening or offer a selection of classic mid-century drinks. Ensure that non-alcoholic options are available for guests who don't consume alcohol.

9. Ambiance Lighting:
  - Use lighting fixtures that capture the mid-century modern aesthetic. Sputnik chandeliers, tripod floor lamps, or pendant lights with clean lines can enhance the atmosphere.

10. Floral Arrangements:
  - Choose floral arrangements with a mid-century vibe. Consider bold blooms like dahlias or tulips in vibrant colors. Place arrangements in sleek vases or mid-century modern-inspired containers.

11. Photo Booth:
  - Set up a photo booth with props reminiscent of the mid-century era. Encourage guests to take fun, retro-style photos as keepsakes from the party.

12. Party Favors:
  - Send guests home with party favors that reflect the theme. Consider small retro-inspired items, vintage-style candies, or personalized mementos.

13. Games and Entertainment:

- Provide entertainment that was popular in the mid-century era. Board games, a vinyl record player, or even a dance floor with music from the era can keep guests engaged.

14. Attention to Detail:

- Pay attention to small details, such as napkin rings, place cards, and centerpieces. These details contribute to the overall cohesiveness of the mid-century modern theme.

15. Guest Interaction:

- Plan activities that encourage guest interaction and conversation. Consider icebreaker games or a themed trivia contest related to mid-century culture.

By incorporating these elements, you can create a memorable and immersive mid-century modern dinner party experience for your guests. The key is to infuse the event with the distinctive style and atmosphere of the mid-20th century while ensuring a modern and enjoyable gathering.

A SUGGESTED PLAYLIST

Here's a suggested 2-hour playlist that leans heavier on jazz,
creating a sophisticated and vibrant atmosphere for your mid-
century modern-themed party:

1. "Take Five" - Dave Brubeck Quartet
2. "Blue Monk" - Thelonious Monk
3. "A Night in Tunisia" - Dizzy Gillespie
4. "So What" - Miles Davis
5. "Fever" - Peggy Lee
6. "Autumn Leaves" - Cannonball Adderley
7. "In the Mood" - Glenn Miller and His Orchestra
8. "My Favorite Things" - John Coltrane
9. "Fly Me to the Moon" - Frank Sinatra
10. "Cantaloupe Island" - Herbie Hancock
11. "Beyond the Sea" - Bobby Darin
12. "Freddie Freeloader" - Miles Davis
13. "Cheek to Cheek" - Ella Fitzgerald and Louis Armstrong
14. "Watermelon Man" - Herbie Hancock
15. "Feeling Good" - Nina Simone
16. "Moanin'" - Charles Mingus
17. "Satin Doll" - Duke Ellington
18. "Don't Explain" - Billie Holiday
19. "Birdland" - Weather Report
20. "L-O-V-E" - Nat King Cole

Feel free to adjust the order or add/subtract songs based on
your preferences and the flow of the party. Enjoy the jazzy
vibes at your mid-century modern-themed gathering!

FURNITURE

Here are 10 pieces of furniture or reproduction items that would complement the mid-century modern theme at your party:

1. Eames Lounge Chair and Ottoman:
- An iconic piece, the Eames Lounge Chair and Ottoman exudes mid-century modern sophistication. Its sleek design and leather upholstery make it a perfect addition to your party.

2. Saarinen Tulip Table and Chairs:
- The Saarinen Tulip Table with its pedestal base and matching chairs featuring tulip-shaped seats is a classic mid-century modern set that adds elegance to your dining or lounge area.

3. Noguchi Coffee Table:
- The Noguchi Coffee Table, designed by Isamu Noguchi, is a sculptural piece with a glass top supported by curved wooden elements. It's a timeless and artistic addition to your space.

4. George Nelson Ball Clock:
- This iconic clock designed by George Nelson is a playful and artistic timepiece that can serve as a decorative element on a wall, adding a touch of mid-century modern charm.

5. Arco Floor Lamp:
- The Arco Floor Lamp, designed by Achille and Pier Giacomo Castiglioni, features a suspended arc and a marble base. Its clean lines and functional design make it a staple in mid-century modern decor.

6. Womb Chair and Ottoman:
- The Womb Chair and Ottoman, designed by Eero Saarinen, is a cozy yet stylish addition to your party space. Its enveloping design and soft upholstery offer comfort and sophistication.

7. Bertoia Diamond Chair:

- The Bertoia Diamond Chair, designed by Harry Bertoia, is a sculptural wire chair that adds a touch of modernist artistry to your seating arrangement.

8. Eames Molded Plastic Rocker:

- The Eames Molded Plastic Rocker is a playful and comfortable rocking chair that can be a quirky addition to your party space, encouraging relaxation and conversation.

9. Mid-Century Modern Sideboard:

- A sleek and minimalist mid-century modern sideboard provides both storage and a stylish display surface. Look for clean lines, tapered legs, and minimalist hardware.

10. Egg Chair:

- The Egg Chair, designed by Arne Jacobsen, is a distinctive and luxurious piece that adds a sculptural element to your space. Its unique shape and swivel base make it a standout seating option.

Remember to mix and match these pieces to create a well-balanced and visually appealing environment that captures the essence of mid-century modern design.

THE READING LIST

If this book is a starting place, here's a reading list that explores mid-century modern cooking and cuisine, offering insights into the culinary trends, recipes, and cultural influences of that era:

1. "Betty Crocker's Picture Cook Book" by Betty Crocker
- A classic from the 1950s, this cookbook provides a glimpse into the popular recipes and cooking styles of mid-century America.

2. "Mastering the Art of French Cooking" by Julia Child
- Julia Child's iconic cookbook, first published in 1961, revolutionized American home cooking by introducing French techniques and recipes.

3. "The Joy of Cooking" by Irma S. Rombauer
- An enduring classic, this cookbook spans several editions and captures the evolving tastes and trends of mid-century American cuisine.

4. "The Escoffier Cookbook and Guide to the Fine Art of Cookery" by Auguste Escoffier
- While originally published in the early 20th century, Escoffier's influence on culinary arts continued into mid-century cooking. This book offers classic French recipes and techniques.

5. "A Treasury of Great Recipes" by Vincent Price
- Actor Vincent Price and his wife Mary collaborated on this cookbook, documenting their culinary adventures and featuring recipes from around the world.

6. "Better Homes and Gardens New Cook Book"
- This iconic cookbook has seen many editions, and each reflects the changing tastes and preferences of mid-century American home cooks.

7. "The Art of Mexican Cooking" by Diana Kennedy

- Diana Kennedy's exploration of Mexican cuisine provides a comprehensive look at the diverse flavors and techniques of this culinary tradition.

8. "The Settlement Cookbook" by Simon Kander

- Originally published in 1901, this cookbook was a staple in many mid-century households, offering a blend of traditional and modern recipes.

9. "American Food: The Gastronomic Story" by Evan Jones

- Evan Jones delves into the history of American cuisine, providing a contextual understanding of mid-century food culture.

10. "The Silver Palate Cookbook" by Julee Rosso and Sheila Lukins

- Although published in the late 1970s, this cookbook influenced home cooking in the 1980s and reflects a departure from traditional cooking styles.

11. "How to Cook a Wolf" by M.F.K. Fisher

- While not exclusively mid-century, Fisher's writing captures the spirit of post-war cooking and the resourcefulness required during that time.

12. "Cooking Price-Wise" by Vincent Price

- Vincent Price's second appearance on this list, this book focuses on budget-friendly recipes while maintaining a sense of elegance.

These books provide a diverse exploration of mid-century modern cooking, from the traditional American fare to the influences of international cuisine. Enjoy your culinary journey through the flavors of the past!

WHY "THE ART OF MEXCIAN COOKING"?

"The Art of Mexican Cooking" by Diana Kennedy is a significant inclusion in the reading list for mid-century modern cooking and cuisine for several reasons:

1. Cultural Exploration:

- Diana Kennedy's book delves into the authentic flavors and techniques of Mexican cuisine. In the mid-20th century, there was a growing interest in exploring and incorporating international flavors into American kitchens, making Kennedy's work particularly relevant.

2. Changing Tastes and Trends:

- The mid-century period saw a shift in culinary preferences, with an increasing appreciation for diverse and global flavors. Kennedy's book captures this shift by introducing readers to the rich and varied world of Mexican cooking.

3. Influence on American Cooking:

- Diana Kennedy's meticulous research and documentation of Mexican culinary traditions had a profound impact on the American culinary landscape. Her work helped elevate Mexican cuisine beyond stereotypes, contributing to its recognition and popularity in the United States.

4. Culinary Education:

- During the mid-century, there was a growing interest in culinary education and exploration. Kennedy's book serves as an educational resource, providing readers with in-depth knowledge about Mexican ingredients, cooking methods, and regional specialties.

5. Culinary Adventurism:

- The mid-century modern era encouraged culinary adventurism and experimentation. Kennedy's exploration of the diverse and complex world of Mexican cuisine aligns with the adventurous spirit of mid-century home cooks seeking new and exciting flavors.

Overall, "The Art of Mexican Cooking" contributes to the broader narrative of mid-century modern cooking by reflecting the era's curiosity about international cuisines and its influence on shaping the American culinary palate.

RECIPE HUNTING

To explore mid-century modern appetizers and desserts, you can refer to a variety of resources that capture the culinary trends and recipes of that era. Here are some suggestions:

1. Vintage Cookbooks:
 - Look for vintage cookbooks from the mid-20th century. Cookbooks published during the 1940s, 1950s, and 1960s often contain a treasure trove of appetizer and dessert recipes popular during that time.

2. Community Cookbooks:
 - Community or church cookbooks from the mid-century often feature recipes submitted by local home cooks. These can provide a glimpse into the types of appetizers and desserts enjoyed in specific regions.

3. Online Recipe Archives:
 - Explore online recipe archives and databases that focus on retro or vintage recipes. Websites dedicated to preserving culinary history may have curated collections of mid-century appetizers and desserts.

4. Food Magazines and Publications:
 - Old issues of popular food magazines from the mid-century, such as "Better Homes and Gardens," "Good Housekeeping," or "Gourmet," can be a source of inspiration. Many of these publications featured seasonal recipes, including appetizers and desserts.

5. Cooking Shows and Videos:
 - Search for cooking shows or videos from the mid-century era. Some classic TV shows featured segments on entertaining and party planning, offering insights into popular appetizers and desserts.

6. Culinary History Books:
- Books that explore the history of American cuisine and culinary trends can provide context and background information on mid-century appetizers and desserts.

7. Library Archives:
- Local libraries or culinary archives may house historical cookbooks and resources that focus on mid-century cooking. Librarians or archivists can assist you in finding relevant materials.

8. Food Blogs and Websites:
- Some food bloggers and culinary historians specialize in recreating and documenting mid-century recipes. Explore their blogs or websites for curated collections and modern adaptations.

9. Social Media Groups:
- Join social media groups or forums dedicated to vintage cooking and mid-century recipes. Members often share their discoveries, recipes, and tips for recreating classic dishes.

10. Vintage Cooking Shows:
- Seek out vintage cooking shows that aired during the mid-century era. Some of these shows featured renowned chefs or home cooks demonstrating popular appetizers and desserts of the time.

Remember to adapt recipes to suit modern tastes and dietary preferences while still preserving the essence of mid-century flavors and presentation.

FINAL WORDS

Revisiting the mid-century modern approach to food, socializing, and dinner parties is not just a journey into culinary
history; it's an exploration of a unique era where creativity,
style, and sophistication converged. As you embark on this
culinary adventure, may your kitchen be filled with the spirit
of mid-century innovation, and may your gatherings be infused
with the charm and elegance that defined an era.

Whether you're recreating classic recipes, experimenting
with vintage cocktails, or curating a playlist that captures the
essence of the times, may your mid-century modern-inspired
endeavors be a delightful blend of nostalgia and contemporary
flair.

Here's to the joy of discovering forgotten flavors, the art of
presentation, and the pleasure of sharing good food with good
company. May your mid-century modern culinary exploration
be a celebration of the past, a nod to the present, and an inspiration for future gatherings.

Wishing you delightful cooking adventures and memorable
moments around the table. Cheers to the timeless appeal of
mid-century modern cuisine!

www.ingramcontent.com/pod-product-compliance
Lightning Source LLC
Chambersburg PA
CBHW051324120626
46547CB00015B/2390